High Agency

How Everyday People Create Extraordinary Outcomes

Caelin Kompass

Table of Contents

TABLE OF CONTENTS

SECTION I:
START HERE

Guiding Principle: Outside of science and law, there are no rules.

Introduction

"We believe that people with passion can change the world for the better."

Steve Jobs, 1997 "Think Different" Campaign Speech

The tragedy isn't that we can't shape our lives.

The tragedy is that we can - we just forgot we're allowed to try.

Most lives are lost in small, polite ways.

One "reasonable" compromise at a time

One "that's just how things are" after another.

One more year of waiting for the right moment, the right permission, the right circumstances.

One more year of realizing that right isn't coming to save you.

Most of us don't crash and burn in some spectacular failure.

We idle. We drift aimlessly.

We're seduced by the promise of safety.

We accept artificial limitations as laws.

Suggestions as commandments.

And then wonder why we're not living the life that, deep down, we know is possible.

The villain is not failure.

The villain is believing the lie that you need the very permission you've had all along.

High agency is reaching the inevitable and unmistakable conclusion — you're the only authority on what's possible for your life.

Nearly everything you've accepted as fixed is actually negotiable.

And once you realize that?

You won't want to go back to learned powerlessness.

Skeptical?

Steve Jobs believed it and said this about it:

"When you grow up you tend to get told that the world is the way it is and your life is just to live your life inside the world.

Try not to bash into the walls too much. Try to have a nice family life, have fun, save a little money.

But life… that's a very limited life.

Life can be much broader once you discover one simple fact and that is: everything around you that you call life was made up by people that were no smarter than you.

And you can change it. You can influence it.

You can build your own things that other people can use.

And the minute that you understand that you can poke life and if you push in something will pop out the other side.

That you can change it.

You can mold it.

That's maybe the most important thing - is to shake off this erroneous notion that life is there and you're just going to live in it versus embrace it, change it, improve it, make your mark upon it...

Once you learn that, you'll never be the same again."

Whether Steve Jobs or I'm right or wrong — suspend your disbelief for a moment — and answer this:

Is this useful?

If you had this belief about life, would it give you more power, authority, and control over your life?

Think about yesterday. Or last week. Or last month.

What did you not do because you assumed you couldn't?

What conversation did you not have because "I can't talk about that?"

What idea or possibility was dead on arrival because of a story you made up in your head about it?

What area of your life did you feel powerless to change? Especially when the only risk was breaking an unspoken "rule" that may have never existed in the first place.

That's low agency.

And it's not your fault.

You've been trained for it since birth.

Every "be realistic," every "stay in your lane," every "that's not how things work" was another bar added to a self-imposed prison you didn't even know you were building.

I'd like for you to consider another possibility — you can be someone that life is happening to... Or... *You can be happening to life.*

George Mack says it beautifully:

> **"Optimism states the glass is half full. Pessimism states the glass is half empty. High agency states you're a tap. You look in the mirror and see a giant tap staring back at you."**

This book is about becoming the tap or a bigger tap.

It's about becoming someone who doesn't simply accept "reality" but actively influences it.

High agency allows you to turn impossibilities into certainties.

Obstacles into opportunities.

Challenges into capabilities.

Setbacks into setups.

"Can I?" into "How do I?"

"You're not allowed to" into "who says?"

"You need permission" into "I already have it."

"Be realistic" into "Your limitations are yours, not mine."

The best part?

It's not some vague set of traits you're either born with or not.

It's learnable.

And if it's learnable, it's improvable.

This means the only limit to how far you can go is up to you.

And I believe this is one of, if not THE, most powerful skill sets you can ever build.

Let's get to it.

How This Book Will Benefit You

WARNING:

This book contains a concept so powerful, so big, so impactful, it can only be used for good or evil. Wield it wisely.

If I asked you, "What are you struggling with right now?" What would you say?

Whatever it is, I'm betting the gap between where you are and where you need to be isn't wishing — it's behavior.

My goal is to show you the specific skills and behaviors that let some people turn "impossible" into "done" while others remain stuck explaining why they can't.

Without different actions, there are no different results. And without results, you haven't really learned anything — at best, you've just been entertained.

My goal is simple: to help show you the skills and behaviors that lead to high agency outcomes.

If you're an achiever — you'll love this book.

Some people build rockets.

Some people build houses.

I build people.

What I've discovered is: There's always a gap between where you are and where you want to go.

Between who you are today and who you envision tomorrow.

Between what your life is like today and what you'd like it to be more like tomorrow.

Maybe you want to:

> Make more money
>
> Improve your relationship
>
> Connect with people more deeply
>
> Escape a stifling job
>
> Start a business
>
> Massively scale your business

Any outcome you want creates the next question: How do you get it?

And if you want to have fun with it:

> What if it were easy?
>
> Or fun?
>
> Or exciting and made you feel alive?
>
> Or any other number of possibilities.

Unfortunately, what happens next stops most people before they start:

I can't because...

That would never work...

It's impossible...

It's not the right time...

My husband or wife wouldn't approve...

It's too risky...

Unfortunately, this is where the conversation ends for many people. That's the cycle they go through over and over.

It's classic *learned powerlessness.*

They want to be happening to life... but instead, life is happening to them, and they act as if they're simply a bystander who has no agency (ability to exert power and authority over their life).

For me, this is the beginning of another conversation:

What stops people?

Why do some people succeed and others fail?

What are the distinctions that separate people who get what they want versus those who don't?

How do some people turn impossibilities into certainties?

What makes some people who hear "No" or "Impossible" stop, while other people simply take it as a suggestion to change their approach?

Yet again, simply knowing these answers doesn't lead to breakthroughs and more importantly - results.

Because let's face it, results are all that matter. (more on that later)

You can logically know what stops people: fear, judgement, ego, lack of belief... you name it.

People will come up with endless reasons to rationalize their lack of results.

As my friend and mentor **Michael Carrigan** says, **"You can have reasons or results."**

Knowing the reasons that stop people isn't enough. You have to go deeper if you want to create possibilities and results.

Your brain is a meaning-making and problem-solving machine.

Better questions → better results

> How do we get unstuck from what stops us?
>
> How do we move through the resistance that holds us back?
>
> How do we remove whatever is stopping us?
>
> How do we create the results and the life we want... and make it easy?

Removing this resistance allows people to achieve more, have more impact, do bigger things, and have a bigger life.

I believe many people simply have missing frameworks for creating the outcomes and life they want.

I also believe the role of a good coach is to help fill those missing structures.

My goal is to provide you with a systematic and structured process to do today what you couldn't do yesterday.

If you want your life to be bigger, richer, and full of possibilities, keep reading.

I believe moving up on the high agency spectrum is one of the most important gifts you can give yourself.

It's also one of the most important gifts you can give those around you, your family, your friends, your community, your peers.

So the question becomes:

What is high agency and how do I move up on the high agency spectrum?

That, my friend, is the central question.

And exactly what this book is going to answer with the explicit goal of:

Helping you systematically build a set of skill sets, traits, identity, beliefs, and behaviors that will move you up the high agency spectrum.

Bending Reality

"Overcome the notion that you must be regular. It robs
you of the chance to be extraordinary."

Uta Hagen

"All I want to know is where I'm going to die so
I'll never go there."

Charlie Munger

If I told you exactly how to fail, what would it be worth to you?

Study successful people or anyone who's where you'd like to be,
and you'll see what they do. But, that doesn't tell the full story.

Oftentimes it's more helpful to invert — to look at what they
don't do.

So to the right person, knowing exactly how to fail would be
incredibly valuable.

They'd just do the opposite.

And serendipity would occur.

Because there are a million ways to succeed.

And incidentally, nearly everyone fails in predictable, copy-paste
ways.

The tragedy? Almost nobody notices. They just keep repeating the same behaviors, convinced their situation is unique.

Meanwhile, there are people with the capability, the drive, the ideas. People who should be winning. But somewhere along the way, they started playing by rules they never agreed to. Now they're stuck watching others with half their talent get twice the results.

These are — **high agency people stuck living low agency lives.**

They know they're capable of more because they ARE capable of more.

The biggest thing holding them back? Agency — the ability to exert power over your life and circumstances.

Here's where it gets interesting. High agency isn't just an idea. It's a set of trainable, actionable skills. Build them, and you don't just play the game differently.

You bend reality.

Gaining Momentum

The concept of high agency exploded into mainstream consciousness recently, particularly through George Mack's viral article that's been viewed by millions.

His work awakened people to this concept — many for the first time — and showed them what high agency looks like and strategies for moving up the spectrum.

This book comes at it from a different angle.

Through years of coaching, I've discovered a common pattern: *capability rarely stops people.* It's usually all the human stuff that stops us.

The emotions, beliefs, fears, desires. The old identities we're protecting while trying to build new ones. The stories we tell ourselves that may or may not be true.

Knowing what high agency looks like isn't enough. Most people can understand the concept perfectly. They can explain every principle. They just can't seem to do it.

Why? Because high agency isn't just a concept. It's rejecting externally imposed limitations. It's refusing to accept other people's definitions of what's possible, normal, or permissible.

The real breakthrough comes when you recognize that you're already free but have been trained to believe you're not.

Which brings me to what often gets missed.

The Human Game

In my experience, humans aren't machines.

We're not input → output.

We have all these emotions, stories, beliefs, conflicting values.

We face what seem like impossible choices.

Stay miserable in a relationship or abandon your kids?

Keep the soul-crushing job or risk your family's security?

Conform to expectations or lose everyone's respect?

Most people think those are the only options.

High agency people?

They find option C — the one that wasn't even on the board.

The High Agency Move

High agency is actually more of an effect of causes than a cause in itself.

If you want to drive it more effectively, you need to understand where that comes from in the first place.

What creates it?

What kills it?

And most importantly: How to build the skills and behaviors.

You can 'know' everything about high agency, but the truth is:

Knowing and doing are universes apart.

That's why this is a behavior change book.

Because without behavior change, nothing changes.

That's why I wrote this book.

I asked - what's the most high agency thing I can do right now?

Write a book in less than 30 days.

Challenge accepted.

Behavior change in action.

And if I can write a book in 30 days, what could you do in the next 30 days?

Let's find out.

High Agency

"It's better to be different than it is to be better. It's also way easier to be different than to be the best. And if you become the ONLY, you're the best by default."

Ian Stanley

High Agency and Low Agency In An Experiment

This experiment terrifies some, awakens others, and hilariously, nearly everyone thinks… "That would never be me."

In 1961 Stanley Milgram conducted an experiment at Yale to test the limits of obedience.

Participants were told to administer electric shocks to a stranger in another room. Each wrong answer meant a stronger shock.

The stranger screamed. Begged. Eventually went silent.

The shocks weren't real but the participants didn't know that.

The wild part?

65% of people administered the maximum, potentially lethal, 450-volt shock.

Why? Because someone in a position of perceived authority told them to.

They weren't evil or cruel. They just couldn't say no to authority.

Here's where it gets fun.

When two other "teachers" complied, compliance jumped to 90%. But what about when just one peer disobeyed?

It dropped to 10%.

It's a masterclass on the importance of *selective disobedience*.

A Rippling Spark

Most people look at this study and think, "How can people comply so easily? That's terrifying."

But look deeper. Look for the potential for positive change.

Imagine being the only person in that room who says "No."

The only one willing to stand up, walk out, and refuse despite every pressure to comply.

All it takes is a spark. One person to exert their personal power, and suddenly others feel permission to push back too.

That's high agency.

It's infectious. Because people living low agency lives are starving for permission to live the high agency lives they know they're capable of.

Defining High Agency

At its core, high agency is:

> **The ability to bend reality to your will despite circumstances, obstacles, consensus, or conventional wisdom.**

Sounds bold? Absolutely. It's difficult to overstate just how powerful this skill set is. It allows you to turn perceived impossibilities into certainties. Where most people see obstacles, high agency people see potential.

It's a fundamental orientation towards your potential — your capacity to turn your desires and dreams into outcomes despite prevailing norms, social constructs, or perceived limitations.

Low agency people:

Accept life as it's presented to them.

Accept other's beliefs about how the world works as their own.

Obey unwritten rules, follow invisible scripts, and mistake suggestions for law.

Have a low ability to exert their will and authority on life.

High agency people:

Push back on life.

Form their own independent conclusions.

Create paths where none existed.

Have a high ability to exert their power and authority on life.

Think of high agency as an operating system that allows people to operate outside the traditional social constructs, to operate independently and exert sovereignty over their life, to interact with reality on a bigger playing field, and creatively find paths unavailable to others.

It's helpful to see how this looks through an experiment.

The Hostile Nation Question

Imagine your plane goes down in a hostile nation. You're the only survivor. No passport. No language. No money. And your phone has just enough battery for one call. Who do you call to save you?

The person you thought of — why them?

It's probably not because they're the richest, the smartest, or the most disciplined. It's because you know they'll figure it out. They'll deal with governments, navigate systems, persuade strangers, improvise solutions, and keep going until you're safe.

That ability — to turn impossibility into inevitability, across domains, under pressure — is high agency.

Conventional wisdom says it can't be done. They make it happen regardless.

And it's equally available to you also.

The fun part?

It's not black or white. Something you have or don't have.

You might be high agency in business and low agency in relationships. Bold at work, compliant with love.

My goal is to help you apply high agency consistently, deliberately, and repeatedly, across all areas of life.

The High Agency Spectrum

High agency exists on a spectrum, just like fitness or wealth. Depending on the situation or time you can be higher or lower.

That's how humans are and why the human side to high agency is so important.

You may be a rockstar in one arena and a dud in another. Or you may have operated with high agency for years to build something and now can't get yourself to push beyond for anything new.

Most people's default is to simply accept where they are.

Moving up the high agency spectrum is directly related to the results you get in life.

Low on the spectrum = no ability to influence your life.

High on the spectrum = creating your future.

The question becomes: Where are you now? And how do you climb higher through specific skills?

The High Agency Ladder

To actually increase your agency — not just understand it — think of it as a ladder you can climb.

At the bottom you may have: Complacency. Compliance. Conformity.

As you move up it, every rung is another step towards greater autonomy and power over your life.

Viewing it this way provides a more concrete way to create and visualize progress.

Built Not Born

High agency isn't a personality trait you're born with. It's not some mystical force reserved for the special few.

It's a set of learnable skills built on specific foundations.

Said another way: *you have agency over your agency.*

You can develop the very thing that develops everything else.

The person you'd call in a hostile nation? They weren't born that way. They built themselves into someone who figures things out. Someone who creates options. Someone who refuses to accept "that's just how it is."

And if they can build it, so can you.

The only thing stopping most of us isn't ability — it's the stories we tell ourselves about our ability.

"I'm not that kind of person."

"I don't have what it takes."

"People like me don't..."

Those aren't facts. They're decisions.

And you can always make a different decision.

Try On A Different Frame

Humans love to try new things on.

We're always trying on new clothes. New hairstyles. Maybe a new watch.

We do it naturally, unconsciously. Testing. Adjusting. Seeing what fits.

How does it look? How does it feel? Do we like how we look or feel with that?

Try this on: You're the one who gets that call. The one everyone knows will figure it out.

How does it feel? Do you like the way you see yourself?

I'll tell you what I see — it suits you. Like it was tailored specifically just for you.

And the beautiful thing about trying on new identities?

If you like how it fits, you can just... keep wearing it.

You're the authority on your life anyway. Always have been.

In the next chapter, I'll show you the hidden engine that actually drives high agency. It explains why some people can transform their lives while others stay stuck despite knowing all the "right" moves.

The Hidden Engine

If you asked me what's the single most important trait that contributes to success, I'd give you one word:

Hunger.

Not intellect. Not talent. Not connections. Not any of the million excuses people make.

Hunger.

When you're truly hungry, you don't care about looking stupid.

When insatiable curiosity drives you, other's opinions become background noise.

Many business owners preach to be emotionless.

That emotions are a business owner's enemy.

Yet it's the emotions that drive the person to do the thing in the first place.

It's the hidden paradox.

It's the difference between the basement genius who can't get themselves to do anything and the high school drop out who builds an empire.

It doesn't help to have a Ferrari if you have no gas.

High Agency Unlock

Here's what separates those who transform their lives from those who stay stuck despite knowing all the "right" moves:

High agency isn't powered by logic. It's powered by emotion.

This is one of the least talked about aspects of high agency yet it may be the most important because without it, nothing else matters.

It's the reason why:

- Brilliant people often accomplish nothing (all intellect, no fire)
- "Dumb" people build empires (all fire, basic navigation)
- Logic alone rarely changes behavior (wrong fuel type)
- Motivation dies quickly (unless it connects to deep emotion)

It's what allows you to push through obstacles and keep going in the face of uncertainty. It's what makes you figure out whatever needs figuring out because NOT doing it isn't an option.

It's the curiosity, desire, frustration, love, joy or any number of emotions that are the spark.

It's the obsession, the competition, the wonder that drives people.

Emotion drives action.

Emotions Decide. Facts Rationalize.

The Wright Brothers didn't fly because they had a good business plan. They flew because they were obsessed — they HAD to pursue flight.

Sara Blakely didn't create Spanx through market analysis. She was pissed that pantyhose sucked. That frustration turned into a billion-dollar company.

Elon Musk's decisions don't always look rational from the outside. He's driven by an emotional need to make humanity multi-planetary. It's that obsession that makes the impossible seem inevitable.

All of these people were first driven by an emotional need that's then later rationalized with logic. But that's post-game analysis. It's not the thing that got them in the game or kept them going.

It's Not Which Emotions — It's How You Use Them

Any emotion can work for or against you.

Fear can paralyze you OR drive incredible preparation.

Anger can blind you OR fuel necessary change.

Anxiety can spiral you OR be a signal for change.

Even love can make you weak OR make you brave.

It's what you do with them that matters. High agency people ask "How can I use this?" instead of "Why is this happening to me?"

They channel whatever they're feeling toward action rather than letting it consume them.

It's not either/or — It's both/and

High agency happens when hunger meets intellect.

Emotion provides the energy. Intelligence provides the navigation. Together, they create unstoppable momentum.

You need both. But without the emotional engine, all the strategies in the world are just theories collecting dust in your head.

I'd bet on someone with: Level 1 smart, Level 10 hunger

Over someone with: Level 10 smart, level 1 hunger

Any day of the week. Twice on Sunday.

It takes hunger to be happening to life.

Because hunger finds a way. Intelligence finds excuses.

Into The Source Code

"Possibility is unavailable to the man who worships
what's wrong."

— Me

The irony plaguing high agency people living low agency lives —
it's rarely hunger that stops them.

They're some of the hungriest people on the planet. They're also
not getting results.

I've been there. You probably have too. It's that special hell where
you're desperate for change, working your ass off, and somehow
still stuck in the same place.

It's one of the worst feelings. Hungry yet fighting yourself. Like
driving with the parking brake on — lots of noise, smoke, and
effort, but you're barely moving.

What I've found is: Hunger without the right source code equals
endless frustration.

You can want it bad enough to taste it. You can grind until you
collapse. But if your underlying operating system is in conflict
with what you're trying to build — you just keep crashing.

Think about it — we all know someone driven who can't seem
to get out of their own way. And we also know some "average
Joe" who keeps winning.

It's the same hunger yet wildly different results.

The difference? Their source code.

What Is Source Code?

Source code is the underlying programming that determines how you process reality and what behaviors emerge. It's your beliefs about what's possible, your identity, your relationship with authority, your values — it's all the invisible architecture that generates visible results.

This is one of the key differences that sets people apart. And it's also one of the areas where people mistakenly try to model visible behaviors and expect a similar result. But it doesn't always work that way.

Copy Success Carefully

Jim Simons, founder of the Renaissance Technologies (hedge fund) died at 86 with an estimated net worth of $31.4 Billion. That's with a B. That's making a million dollars — 31,400 times.

Want to know his success secrets?

- He woke up at 3am.
- Practiced OMAD for mental focus (one meal a day).
- Religiously did a 10 minute ice bath.
- Meditated 20 minutes twice a day.

Just kidding...

He chain-smoked through meetings, walked barefoot around the office, and never exercised. If you copy his habits, you won't get rich. But you might get lung cancer.

The Cause and Effect Trap

A common mental trap is to confuse cause and effect. This is why studying success can be dangerous. We confuse what successful people do with what made them successful.

It looks like this:

Basketball players are tall. If I play basketball, that will make me tall also.

False.

You're more likely to play basketball because you're tall, not because basketball makes you tall.

The same confusion happens with high agency. We see the effects and think they're causes.

This is an important distinction because if you want to develop high agency and have it "stick," it's not always enough to model surface level behavior.

While behavior is what matters — it's the only thing that creates results — we all know it rarely lasts beyond the moments of inspiration.

A deeper shift is needed to anchor lasting change.

The Human Side Of High Agency

High agency isn't just something you do. It's something that emerges. It's an expression of an underlying source code.

You can white-knuckle your way through most things for a week. But without updating the underlying source code, most people just bounce back to who they were.

It's why 92% of people fail their with New Years resolutions. They're trying to willpower their way against an identity they're still holding on to and haven't updated.

My experience as a professional coach and consultant is that capability rarely stops people. It's usually all the human stuff that stops us.

You know, all the: emotions, beliefs, fears, desires. The old identities we're protecting while trying to build new ones. The stories we tell ourselves that may or may not be true. One moment we're catastrophizing, the next we're filled with possibility.

Here's the conflict:

Try to "be more disagreeable" without changing your beliefs about disagreement? You'll just feel like an asshole.

Your identity says you're a peacekeeper — how do you keep the peace while also pushing back against consensus?

What about your emotional associations with rejection?

How could you possibly be disagreeable if every part of you identifies as someone who needs everyone's approval?

You can't.

Which is why updating your source code along the way matters as much as taking action.

The Internal Drivers

The key to consistently climbing the high agency ladder is to update your source code along the way.

A big mistake people make along the way is trying to simply grind harder even when it's not getting results.

My goal is to show you the real drivers behind high agency so that when you hit a sticking point, you can blast through it and keep going.

You don't need to copy anyone else's exact code. You just need to understand the structure well enough to write your own.

In the next chapter, I'll show you that structure. Six components that generate high agency naturally when they're aligned. Not rules to follow, but principles to build from.

The Source Code

What separates high agency people from everyone else?

It's not intelligence — I know plenty of brilliant people who stay stuck forever.

It's not resources — some of the highest agency people I've met started with nothing.

It's not even luck — though high agency people seem to always be luck-maxxing.

It's the source code running underneath everything they do.

Everyone has beliefs, emotions, values, identity. You've got them. I've got them. The difference is how they're configured.

Most people are still running the default programming society installed. High agency people aren't. They've either consciously built or stumbled upon a distinctly different way of operating.

This isn't about having MORE of these things. It's about having different versions. Versions that generate results instead of circular thinking.

When you work with people like I do and you're around enough high agency people you start to notice patterns. These are commonalities that distinctly set people apart. I've noticed these same six components show up again and again. This is the deeper architecture or structure that generates high agency behaviors more naturally.

But, don't get lost in theory here. This isn't philosophy class. I'm going to keep this simple and brief so you can recognize the patterns and use them.

If something resonates, run with it. If not, discard it. Remember, there are many different ways to get what you want and only a few common ways people fail.

Lastly, these all exists on a continuum. It's not — do you have it or not — but to which degree. How much of it do you have or how strongly do you have it. Humans aren't binary. It's not — do we love? It's how deeply. It's not, what do we believe, but how strongly do we believe.

Here are the six source code patterns I've seen most consistently.

1. Hunger

High agency people aren't more emotional than anyone else — they just refuse to live in apathy.

Call it drive, call it obsession, call it hunger — the label doesn't matter. What matters is that something inside them won't let them coast.

I'd wager you've felt this before: the frustration so strong you had to fix it, the curiosity that kept you awake, the desire that made obstacles irrelevant. That's hunger.

I'm covering it first because it's so important.

Without it, you could have the clearest strategies or best plans and they'd mean nothing.

With it and even imperfect action creates momentum.

The opposite of hunger is apathy and complacency — the true kiss of death. That's where dreams go to die. If you feel nothing strongly enough to move, you stay stuck.

Find whatever activates that hunger in you and do more of that.

You won't find a high agency person without it.

2. Beliefs

Everyone has beliefs. The difference is high agency people run different software.

The default for most people is to never question theirs — they wear beliefs like hand-me-down clothes, passed down from parents, teachers, or society. But, high agency people don't passively accept beliefs this way. They question and push back if it's not serving them. I've found they often look at beliefs through the lens of: is this useful?

The limiting belief trap

Too many people think they need to "fix" their beliefs before they can act. They want to launch the business but feel unworthy. They want wealth but believe money is evil. So they wait, thinking they need perfect alignment before they take action.

Don't worry — if you've fallen into this before, you're not alone. I have too. It's almost a seductive form of procrastination.

And then I realized: **The belief that you must fix all your conflicting beliefs before acting is the limiting belief.**

What's different about high agency people? They don't buy into it. They've built a meta-belief that trumps the rest:

Results come from behavior, not from my internal state.

That one belief can change everything if you'll let it.

Low agency: "I feel uncertain, so I can't act."

High agency: "I feel uncertain… and I'm acting anyway."

The marketplace doesn't reward beliefs. It rewards behavior. Your customers don't care about your impostor syndrome — they care about what you deliver. Your boss doesn't need to know about your self-doubt — they care about your performance.

You don't have to feel ready. You don't have to resolve every contradiction. You have to simply start taking behaviors aligned with your direction, then reinforce new beliefs along the way.

Think of it like this: most people stop taking action because their old beliefs get in the way. Action doesn't require perfect beliefs — but rewiring them along the way helps to ensure that yesterday's ceiling is today's floor.

Beyond this, questioning your base assumptions is how you see what others miss. That's what lets you act differently, and get different results. High agency people refuse to blindly accept "that's just how it is." It's that refusal that allows them to operate outside of what most people believe is possible.

A helpful frame can be to view beliefs as levers. They can be tools to help you get results or that hold you back.

For example: if you believe "people are willing to help," you'll ask more questions, make more requests, and open more doors.

If you believe "no one ever helps me," you won't ask at all. You'll prove yourself right but at what costs?

One belief unlocks possibility, the other locks it down.

Most people's beliefs keep them in check — play it safe, don't stand out, wait your turn. High agency beliefs free them to act — problems are solvable, rules are bendable, action creates clarity.

That's why they behave differently. It's also why they get rewarded differently.

At the end of the day, beliefs are a core component of source code that influence your behavior. Change the code and you'll find actions flow more naturally. Leave the defaults in place and you'll often keep stalling.

3. Identity

Most people think identity is discovered. "Finding yourself." "Being true to who you are."

High agency people know identity is constructed. You're not finding yourself — you're building yourself.

This isn't meant to be feel-good philosophy. It's meant to be useful. Whatever you attach "I am" to, you become.

Unfortunately, most people's default is to treat identity as if it's permanent, unchangeable, and inherited.

But it doesn't have to be that way.

High agency people's identity usually revolves around possibility.

It's not only who they are today but also who they choose to build themselves into tomorrow.

I could write an entire book on this alone but here are several key things that allow them to resist against all the social pressures that keep so many people stuck.

Self-permissioning:

High agency people have given themselves permission at the identity level. They don't need the external validation others do because their identity says: "I'm allowed to want this. I'm allowed to try. I'm allowed to fail."

On the other side, most people's default says: "I can't do that, it's not me."

This is the difference between staying stuck and breaking through. Between accepting consensus and pushing back. Between ordinary results and extraordinary ones.

Anti-Fragile by Design

Low agency identities break under pressure. One failure and "I'm an entrepreneur" becomes "I'm a failure."

High agency identities get stronger under pressure. They've built in anti-fragility:

> "Setbacks are just setups."

> "Failure is part of getting good."

> "I grow through discomfort."

Challenges make them stronger and more resilient.

It's a distinctly different way of operating compared to most people who crumble under similar circumstances.

The Live Player Paradigm

Most people play by the rules they're given. High agency people recognize they can rewrite the rules themselves.

They're not just playing the game better — they're changing what game is being played. This requires an identity that says: "I'm not bound by how things have always been done."

It's why when everyone says "that's impossible," their identity says "Who says?"

They simply don't accept limitations the way most people do.

It's the backbone that allows them to withstand the pressure of social pressure betting against them.

This is one of the biggest struggles of entrepreneurs because everyone is telling them to just be realistic and go get a job but their identity pushes through that until they're the ones giving people jobs.

The highest agency people I know and work with all have a sense of identity that's so certain, so strong, that it allows them to seemingly bend reality to their will.

They're live players in their life and refuse to be deterred.

And without that sense of identity, they would've buckled to the pressure long ago.

The great news is — it's not whether you have it or not. It's how willing are you to develop it into who you need to be to get the life you want?

4. Mind Control

One of the most important aspects of high agency is immunity to mind viruses.

The news says recession, everyone panics. The crowd goes left, everyone follows.

High agency people don't. They think their own thoughts, reach their own conclusions, trust their own judgment regardless of external pressure.

This is what allows them to break from consensus and get extraordinary results.

The Basics

Mind control isn't some mystical Jedi trick. It's essentially cognitive agency — your ability to direct your own mental operating system.

The Levers:

Attention control: You choose what to focus on

Meaning-making: You decide what things mean

Significance weighting: You determine how important it is

Frame creation: You build the lens through which you see

Questioning assumptions: You decide what's real

It's why two people can get fired and one spirals into depression and the other starts a business the next day.

Same event. Different mind control. Wildly different outcomes.

Breaking Invisible Prisons

Most people don't realize how much of their thinking isn't actually theirs.

Parent's fears masquerading as "wisdom." Friend's limitations accepted as truth. Cultural norms adopted without question.

They're running someone else's mental software and wondering why they get someone else's results.

On the other hand, high agency people ask:

Who decided this?

Do I actually believe this?

Does this serve me?

They've discovered that most "truths" are just popular opinions. Most "impossible" things are just untested. Most "rules" are just suggestions that got repeated enough.

The Cost of Consensus

For most, it's easier to outsource their thinking. Safer to go with consensus. More comfortable to let others decide what's true.

High agency people *can't* do that. Something in them rebels against passively accepting what's presented without inspecting it first.

Without cognitive agency, you're stuck with borrowed dreams, inherited limitations, and secondhand conclusions.

With it, you can see opportunities others miss. Question assumptions others accept. Create solutions others say are impossible.

All high agency people have this independent judgment. It's what allows them to think differently, act differently, and get dramatically different results.

Because if you think like everyone else, you'll get what everyone else gets.

And you and I both know — you want more than that.

5. Personal Autonomy

We all have inputs in our lives. Parents, friends, experts, society. They're all convinced they know what's best for us.

High agency people listen. Then they decide for themselves. And this is a distinctly different source code than many people have.

Personal autonomy is recognizing you're the final authority on your life. You always have been.

There's a subtle but crucial difference between mind control and autonomy. Mind control is about arriving at your own independent conclusions. Autonomy is knowing you have the RIGHT to.

It's the difference between driving a car and owning it. One is operation, the other is authority.

Your family thinks your career pivot is insane? Mind control helps you reframe their concern as love. Autonomy means you don't need their approval to proceed.

The doctor's opinion? The expert's study? Your parent's wisdom? All valuable input. But you're the ultimate decision-maker.

It's why high agency people feel like they have fundamental authority over:

What paths they take regardless of expectations

What rules they follow that may simply be social constructs

Their right to pursue what they want

The difference between low autonomy and high autonomy is you stop asking "Am I allowed?" and start asking "Do I choose?"

You realize most "authorities" are just people playing roles. Most "rules" are made up things. And most "impossible" things are just someone else's opinion.

Want to triple your prices? Start a business? Switch careers at 45? You'll need autonomy.

People will tell you "you can't."

They'll say "no one does it that way."

They'll list every reason why you don't have the right.

And without autonomy, you'll believe them. With it, you'll make your own decision.

Look, the marketplace will tell you if it works. Reality will let you know. But if you don't exercise autonomy over your own life, you're letting everyone else run it for you.

And they don't have to live with the results. You do.

6. Value(s)

This may be one of the most underrated source code components that's also super important.

Ask ten people their values — family, security, success, freedom — and you'll hear the same words.

So if the words are the same, why do some people get radically different results?

Because the difference between low agency and high agency isn't what they value. It's how they pursue it.

Same Values, Different Strategy

Take security. Everyone wants it.

Low agency approach: "I'll stay in this job I hate because it's stable."

High agency approach: "I'll build multiple income streams so I'm never dependent on one source."

Same value. Completely different execution.

Or family:

One person says "I can't take risks because I have kids."

Another says "I must take risks because I have kids."

Both love their families. They just go about taking care of them differently.

When Values Compete

Here's where it gets interesting. We all have multiple values, and sometimes they conflict.

Want growth AND comfort?

Connection AND independence?

Security AND freedom?

The difference is in what people optimize for.

Low agency people tend to choose:

Comfort over growth

Approval over being real

Certainty over possibility

High agency people tend to choose:

Growth over comfort

Being real over approval

Possibility over certainty

And the difference over time is massive.

It's part of the paradox: because high agency people optimize for results, they usually end up getting the very things low agency people cling to. Comfort. Security. Connection. They just arrive as a byproduct of pursuing possibility.

The Rules You Make

Taking it a step beyond the values themselves, the rules you create matter also.

Two people both value integrity.

One defines it as never changing their mind.

The other says it's admitting when you're wrong.

Or loyalty.

To one person it means never voicing concerns.

To the other it means being honest even when it's uncomfortable.

Again, same values. Different rules. Different life.

High agency people are constantly updating their rules when they find better ways. Low agency people argue for their limitations and wonder why things aren't working out.

Examined vs. Inherited

Most people never question why they actually value what they value. They just inherit a set of things they're supposed to care about and never stop to ask: Do I actually want this?

High agency people do. They take ownership of their values. They don't let other people's priorities dictate their lives.

The key distinction here is that the values may look the same on the surface, but they lead to wildly different results in life.

My goal here is to show you the source code difference between low agency and high agency. We all have these six components, it's just a matter of how much and direction.

Don't get lost in the theory. The point is simple: High agency people run different software than the default programming most people never question.

And you can update your source code. It's not fixed. It's not permanent. It's choice by choice, belief by belief, action by action.

Next, I'll show you the eight distinct skills that emerge when this source code is running. These are the practical, observable behaviors you can start implementing in your own life — fast.

SECTION II: HIGH AGENCY SKILLS

Introduction:
High Agency Behaviors

If you're like me, at this point you're asking, "Do I have high agency?"

I know what it looks like. I understand the source code. But do I have it? And if I don't, what do I actually DO to increase it?

The answer is: High agency is ultimately about behavior. That's the end result.

We all know that person who creates possibilities from thin air. Who turns disasters into opportunities. Who seems to magically make things happen while everyone else explains why they can't.

But what we see are just the outputs. The results of what they've done.

I wish I could tell you an airy fairy story that if you just chant affirmation to yourself in the mirror that your life will change. But that's not how reality works.

It's what you DO that matters.

The positive thinking movement has almost been a trojan horse by misdirecting from the real target of results. People feel like they're making progress without actually changing their circumstances.

It's a classic low agency trap.

The real real is: No Mr. Positive Thinking is coming to save you. No amount of philosophizing from your couch actually changes anything.

You don't have to feel good about it. Plenty of people don't feel the way they thought they would after accomplishing a big goal. But no one wins a Super Bowl through thoughts alone.

High agency is the end result of certain skills all coming together to create something greater than the sum of their parts.

The Power of Combination

A Belgian draft horse can pull about 4,000 pounds alone. Basically your car.

Put two together, and logic says 4,000 + 4,000 = 8,000 pounds.

Nope.

Two Belgian horses together pull 16,000 pounds.

And here's where it gets fun.

Take those same two horses. Let them live together. Eat together. Work together. Build trust. Now they pull 32,000 pounds.

Double. Just from relationship.

The world record? Two Belgian brothers who grew up together.

52,000 pounds.

From 8,000 (what they should pull) to 52,000 (what they actually pulled).

That's a 6.5x multiplier. Not from getting stronger. From working in sync.

The Belgian Horse Effect

High agency skills work the same way. Each one on its own is powerful, but in combination they become something entirely different.

I've identified eight core skills that, when developed together, create that Belgian Horse Effect. Eight specific, learnable behaviors that generate extraordinary results.

Not because each one is special in isolation.

But because having all eight — even at moderate levels — creates a multiplication effect. The outputs far exceed the inputs.

These eight skills are rarely found in combination together at the right levels.

But, the people who have all eight above the threshold? Those are the ones you'd call if you were stranded in a hostile nation. The ones who bend reality and make their own luck. The ones happening to life instead of letting life happen to them.

The Skills Continuum

These skills aren't switches you flip. They're more like dials.

You're not "obsessed" or "not obsessed." You're somewhere on the continuum. Maybe a 3/10. Maybe a 7/10. But you're somewhere.

Same with all skills.

Maybe your calibrated thinking is dialed to a 3 while your resilience is cranked to an 8. You keep getting back up, keep trying, but you're not learning from mistakes as quickly as you could.

A solid 6 across all eight beats being a 10 at two and missing the rest. Turn just a few dials up, and results dramatically shifts.

This isn't about being perfect at all of them, all the time. It's just getting them to the necessary level and that's where the magic happens.

The multiplication effect kicks in. And that's when things get interesting.

Behavior Trumps All

To be explicitly clear: all of these skills require you to do something.

The eight skills I've identified? They're not ideas to think about. They're things to DO.

All the understanding in the world won't move your life forward an inch. Only behavior moves things. Only what you actually do creates results.

I've watched brilliant people stay stuck for years because they understood everything perfectly. They could explain every concept under the sun better than me. They just never did anything about it.

And I've watched "less smart" people smoke all the "intelligent" ones because they just started doing things. Messy. Imperfect. But doing.

The Multiplication Effect

Each of these skills is independently important. People naturally gravitate towards some more than others but the magic is in developing all of them.

If one's too low, it creates a bottleneck.

But when all eight are humming, even at moderate levels?

That's when multiplication kicks in and sparks begin to fly.

The sum becomes greater than the parts. Way greater.

That's when impossible things start happening.

That's when people start calling you lucky.

That's when you start *happening to life.*

Skill One: Obsession

"When I first started studying other obsessive types who were super successful and stopped seeking advice from those who were settling for average lives, average results, average money, average everything and who were never obsessed with anything except defending average, that's when I began to really live."

— Grant Cardone

Obsession isn't a thing you have. It's a thing you do.

Some say it's a personality trait — you either have it or you don't. I disagree. It's a thing you do. And it's a skill you can build through reinforcement and repetition.

One of the traits I value most in the people I surround myself with is obsession. And I call it a trait because it's a persistent behavior.

If someone wants to work with me and I don't feel they have enough of this drive, no matter how lucrative, I decline. Every time.

Why? Because I can't help someone get results who isn't willing to go the distance for themselves.

Here's the difference: One business owner is "interested" in growing profits but won't change their behavior to make it happen. Another with high agency obsession will DO almost anything to increase their bottom line.

If obsession were some inborn trait, you'd have no control — like your height. But if it's a skill, you can improve it. We all know someone who didn't have it, then one day a switch flipped and they did.

Whether I'm right or wrong doesn't matter. It's more useful to treat it like you have control over it. Because then you do.

Answer this: Can you imagine someone rescuing you from a hostile nation without being obsessed about it?

Without it, they wouldn't have developed the skills to make that difference in the first place.

Active Pursuit. Not Passive Interest.

Obsession isn't just a feeling. It's what happens when no one's looking.

Low agency people feel interested. High agency people *behave* obsessed.

One person thinks about it. The other can't stop *doing* things about it.

Obsession Is Trainable

Most people think obsession is something you stumble into. It doesn't have to be. It can also be something you build.

Here's how:

You start doing something — anything — with slightly more attention than usual. You notice when you do it well. That small hit of satisfaction? That's the beginning.

Keep noticing. Keep raising your standard. What was "good enough" yesterday becomes unacceptable today.

This is how a mechanic who doesn't care becomes the guy who can't sleep if a bolt isn't torqued right. How a writer who hates writing becomes someone who can't NOT write.

The military understands this. Not every person who joins is naturally obsessed. They build them. First it's bed corners. Then boots. Then mission. By the end, excellence isn't a choice — it's compulsion.

You can train this yourself. Pick something you do regularly. Anything. Raise your standard by 10%. Notice when you hit it. Feel that micro-win. Tomorrow, raise it again.

Before long, mediocrity will physically bother you. You won't be able to half-ass it anymore.

That's not a personality trait. That's conditioning. And it's completely within your control.

Ungovernable Urgency

This isn't impatience. It's something deeper.

High agency people have an almost fanatical sense of urgency tempered with extreme patience for the long game. They build in 10 years what others couldn't in 50.

They move at breakneck speed while holding a vision that takes decades.

And they don't need a "why."

Ask them why they're driven and maybe they know. Maybe they don't. Doesn't matter.

Their ungovernable urgency is the reason.

It's what separates dabbling from obsession. Dabblers need constant prodding, oversight, reinforcement. The obsessed need restraint. They have to be told to stop, not to start.

Unreasonable Standards

One way to spot high agency obsession: Their floor exceeds most people's ceiling.

It's not about perfectionism — perfectionists procrastinate. It's simply pushing beyond what most consider possible.

For one, it's shipping the book in 30 days because timing matters.

For another, it's taking two years to craft something timeless.

There is no right way here. Context matters. Regardless, their baseline of what's possible exceeds the floor of most others.

The Compound Effect

High agency obsession leads to several distinct outcomes.

Self-taught mastery - Gatekeepers slow them down, so they learn to learn. They break through barriers others accept as necessary.

Rapid skill acquisition - The more skills you learn, the faster you get at learning. Two people can be 40 years old — one has 10X the capabilities. Who do you think was obsessed?

Inspiration activation - Your obsession ignites something dormant in others. They see you chasing something real and remember they could too. You become proof that settling is a choice, not a requirement.

Interesting by default - When you're genuinely obsessed, you become fascinating without trying. You have unique thoughts, unexpected knowledge, stories nobody else has. You become the person people can't get enough of.

Mission magnetism - People are starving to be part of something that matters. Your obsession gives them a mission to join. Like how Elon's Mars vision attracts top talent willing to work insane hours. The mission becomes the magnet.

Reality distortion field - Your certainty about what's possible starts affecting others. They begin believing things they dismissed as impossible, just because your obsession makes it seem inevitable.

The Low Agency Obsession Trap

A low agency trap is to get stuck in obsession as a form of escape.

There's productive obsession and there's elegant procrastination.

Reading your 47th business book without starting a business? That's not obsession. That's creative avoidance.

High agency obsession has a filter: Results.

If your obsession isn't producing outcomes, it's just an expensive hobby.

Obsession is Aliveness

We feel most alive when we're in pursuit of something.

One of the biggest problems I hear from successful people who've "made it" is feeling complacent. They built the thing. Climbed the mountain. Now what?

They've lost that edge. That hunger. The aliveness that comes from obsession.

They're complacent and miserable for it.

It's why they hire a coach and actively seek out others who are hungry.

They're looking to reactivate that sense of pursuit and regain the aliveness they've lost.

Activate Your Obsession

Activating your obsession starts with giving yourself permission to suspend all the false beliefs holding it back and let yourself feel excited about something again.

Hell, I can be excited when I feel a deep anger rise in me over watching someone else beat me in business. It's fuel. My competitiveness is reactivated and I double-down.

If I feel like I'm losing an edge, I'll go walk through the mall. Everyone is walking slow. Everyone going about their life slow.

Everyone is casual about their life.

And it wakes something up in me. I don't want to be casual. I don't want to be complacent. I'm out here with a sense of urgency and I've got places to go, things to build, and a life to live.

My point here is that you don't have to wait for it to strike. You can train it. Start positively reinforcing yourself for what you want more of. Before long, you'll be obsessed with continuing that behavior.

What activates yours? Could be competition. Could be a new possibility. Could be proving someone wrong.

Ultimately, there's no right way. Whatever it is. Use it.

Skill Upgrade

If the opposite of obsession is apathy, can you imagine that person rescuing you from a hostile nation?

They'd be like: "Sorry man, I don't really care enough to try."

The obsessed? "Embassy notified. Called a Navy SEAL buddy. Flying down in five hours."

That's the difference.

Turn this dial up on your life and watch how things start to move.

You don't need permission to be obsessed. You just need to start conditioning yourself to do obsessed things.

And once you start, you might find you can't stop.

Skill Two:
Strategic Non-Conformity

"Reality is negotiable. Outside of science and law, all rules can be bent or broken, and it doesn't require being unethical."

— Tim Ferriss

When you're a kid, you get rewarded for following all the rules.

When you're an adult, you get rewarded for breaking many of the rules other adults are still following.

Learning to bend or break the rules is one of the most valuable skills you can develop.

One thing you'll notice with all high agency people is they seem to operate outside of the rules that most of society accepts.

From the outside it seems as though the rules don't apply to them but in reality, they've just mastered the art of knowing which rules to bend or break and when.

And the result is that society disproportionately rewards them for it.

Shovels Are Greater Than Gold

In 1849, James Marshall found gold at Sutter's Mill. Within months, 300,000 people abandoned everything to chase their fortune in California.

Samuel Brannan heard the same news. But instead hopping on the speculation train, he bought every shovel, pick axe, and pan in the region.

Then he ran through San Francisco shouting "Gold! Gold! Gold from the American River!"

He opened a supply store. Marked everything up 1000% and made $150,000 in nine weeks. That's about $5 million today.

He became California's first millionaire. Ironically, he never even touched a nugget of gold.

300,000 people had the same information. Only one person thought differently. That's strategic non-conformity: seeing the option everyone else's brain won't generate.

> **"Discovery consists of seeing what everyone has seen and thinking what nobody has thought."**
>
> **— David Ogilvy**

The Insight

Strategic non-conformity isn't just being disagreeable. It's three things:

First, you have to THINK the thought. Most people's brains won't even generate certain options. They've erected guardrails that kill ideas before they form.

Second, you have to JUDGE it independently. Even if the thought occurs, most people kill it with "but what will people think?" High agency people ask "will this work?" not "is this allowed?"

Third, you have to ACT strategically. Not every rule is worth breaking. Not every battle is worth fighting. You have to know when conforming costs nothing and when it costs everything.

Brannan could think "sell shovels not dig for gold," judge it as brilliant despite everyone doing the opposite, then act on it while 300,000 people chased gold.

Science, Law, or Story?

Most of the things that stop us aren't science or law. They're social constructs we've failed to challenge. They're just stories we've created about what we can or can't do.

If it doesn't violate science or law, then it's negotiable.

There are endless stories of people who simply decided they wanted to do something, then went and did it while everyone else is telling themselves a story of why they can't.

What's Your Compliance Costing You?

Every rule you follow has a cost. Most people never calculate it.

Wearing a suit to the meeting? Costs nothing, might open doors. Smart conformity.

Accepting industry pricing? Costs millions in lost revenue. Expensive compliance.

Following "proper channels"? Costs months waiting for permission you may not even need.

"That's just how business is done here"? Costs your competitive advantage if you don't innovate.

High agency people know when agreeableness is cheap and when it's bankrupting them.

The Guardrails in Your Head

We've been trained to be so agreeable, so compliant, that we self-censor before anyone else needs to.

Oftentimes, people we call resourceful simply allow themselves to generate options beyond what others find acceptable.

A key to this skill set is to dismantle these guardrails. You have to let yourself run with creativity. Ask questions that force you to come up with unreasonable answers. You'll see just how far this can go.

High agency people oftentimes see options that aren't even on the board for others. There are plenty of them that are no smarter than you, only they removed the guardrails preventing them from seeing greater options.

The Disagreeability Dial

High agency people don't disagree with everything all the time. They're selective, especially when the risk/reward works in their favor.

They're capable of disagreeability but use it strategically.

We've all met the person who's disagreeable about everything. They're assholes. We've also met the people pleaser who's overly agreeable.

The key is being capable yet knowing when to exercise that disagreeability.

High agency people are surprisingly agreeable, charismatic, and moving at times. They can push people yet also know when to pull them.

This allows them to spot opportunities others don't see while also building teams around them.

It's not a binary either/or. It's a dial that can be tuned depending on what's necessary.

And of course, the measuring stick is results.

Zig When Others Zag

Jeff Bezos quit his Wall Street job to sell books online. Everyone said he was insane. Throwing away guaranteed success for internet nonsense.

He wasn't being rebellious. He saw an option others couldn't see, judged it superior despite consensus, and acted on it.

That's not simple disagreeability. That's the ability to think independently, evaluate clearly, and move decisively when everyone else is frozen by groupthink.

The Multiplication Effect

When strategic non-conformity combines with the other seven skills, impossible things start happening.

Your obsession finds paths others can't see. Your resilience pushes through where others would stop. Your frame control makes your "crazy" idea seem inevitable.

Without this skill, you're playing by rules that winners already broke. With it, you're playing an entirely different game.

The person you'd call from behind enemy lines? They're not following the proper channels. They're not waiting for permission. They're not accepting "that's impossible."

They're thinking thoughts others won't allow themselves to think, judging them without needing approval, and acting while everyone else is still asking "are we allowed to do that?"

That's the difference between life happening to you and you happening to life.

The rules you think are real? Most of them are just stories. And you can change them whenever you decide.

Skill Three:
Brutal Honesty &
Productive Delusion

"There are two ways to be fooled. One is to believe what isn't true; the other is to refuse to believe what is."

– Soren Kierkegaard

Nine days before the Wright Brothers flew, the New York Times published an article declaring that humans wouldn't achieve powered flight for one to ten million years.

The Times wasn't alone. Simon Newcomb, renowned astronomer, had just mathematically "proven" human flight violated the laws of physics.

But, that wasn't going to stop two bicycle mechanics from Ohio.

December 14, 1903: Wilbur Wright pilots their flying machine off the launch rail. Three and a half seconds later, he nose-dives into the sand.

Damage report: Flying machine? Minor. Ego and confidence? Major.

The brothers had been at this for four years. Spent their life savings. Been mocked by the press when they bothered to cover them at all.

The honest assessment: "We flew for 3.5 seconds then crashed. Our design still has flaws."

The productive delusion: "We'll fly tomorrow."

Not in a million years. Tomorrow.

Three days later, while the Times article was still in circulation, they flew for 59 seconds and covered 852 feet.

This was the first controlled and sustained flight in history. All because they had brutal honesty and productive delusion.

This is the *paradox* of high agency — **being completely honest about current reality while maintaining unreasonable belief about what's possible.**

Everyone "knew" human flight was impossible. The Wright Brothers knew everyone was wrong.

They held both truths: honest acknowledgment of each failure, delusional certainty of eventual success.

Two Truths, One Person

High agency people hold two contradictory truths without breaking.

They'll tell you their business is failing AND that it'll be worth millions. They know they can't code AND they're building the next big app. They admit this attempt failed AND believe the next attempt will work.

Most people can't do this. They either lie about reality or give up on possibility.

I see it constantly. Someone will say "I know I'll be successful" while refusing to look at their results. Or they'll be so "realistic" about their current situation they won't even try.

Neither leads to the type of success achievers want.

Why Both Are Essential

Brutal honesty alone isn't enough. You see every problem, every gap, every reason it won't work. And you get to be "right" about everything except what matters — that you could change it.

This is the eternal pessimist.

Pure delusion alone makes you crash repeatedly into the same walls. You never learn because you won't acknowledge what isn't working.

But together? That's how impossible happens.

The Wright Brothers needed honesty to learn from each crash. They needed productive delusion to keep building after each crash.

It takes both to accomplish impossible goals.

The Behavior Test

Behavior is what separates delusion from productive delusion.

Regular delusion: "I'll be successful someday" while scrolling Instagram.

Productive delusion: "I'll be successful" paired with "I need 1000 sales calls to get good" followed by actually making the calls.

A big possibility only becomes reality when backed up by the action necessary.

Without action, you're just another person with dreams. With action, you're building evidence along the path of what many people would say is just a pipe dream.

How This Looks In Real Life

You might be a business owner who wants to 10X his or her bottom line and so far nothing has worked.

Brutal honesty: This approach isn't working.

Productive delusion: The right approach will work.

You need both to keep pushing forward.

Most continue with failing strategies rather than cutting losses and trying something new.

I see it all the time — people would rather be "right" than accept the truth of where they're at. And unfortunately, it stops them from where they could be.

You Don't Need Evidence First

A low agency trap is to want evidence before it's created. It's like saying: *Once I'm good at business, I'll start a business.*

You have to start the business to get good at it.

You need the productive delusion to believe it'll work before you have evidence it does

The Wright Brothers had proof of the opposite — every attempt in history had failed. Experts with credentials said it was impossible. The math said it wouldn't work.

High agency doesn't wait for evidence. It creates it.

Each crash taught them something (honesty). Each rebuild got them closer (action). The delusion kept them building (persistence).

They didn't stack evidence until they believed. They believed, then stacked evidence until it was true.

Holding The Tension

You know that uncomfortable feeling when you're failing but still telling people you'll succeed?

I've been there before multiple times and it sucks. I've also watched countless people throw the towel in on their dreams at this point.

This is why entrepreneurship feels crazy — you have to be delusional enough to believe you'll succeed while honest enough to see where you're currently failing.

You have to be a little bit crazy to pursue what you believe in despite the monumental hurdles business owners face each day.

It's why high agency is so vital to businesses: having the capability of holding "this isn't working" and "it will work" at the same time.

It's in this valley of despair where low agency people see impossible and high agency people make it possible.

Making It Practical

Pick something you want but think you can't have or do.

Now be brutally honest:

> What skills are you missing?

> What resources don't you have?

> What's actually in your way?

Write it down. All of it. Don't sugar-coat.

Now maintain productive delusion: You'll figure out every single one of those problems.

Not because you have evidence. Because you'll create evidence through attempts.

That's what the person you'd call stranded in a hostile nation would do. Face exactly how bad the situation is, believe completely they'll solve it, then start making calls.

Your Choice

You can be honest about where you are and accept it as permanent. That's one choice.

You can be delusional about where you are and never improve. That's another.

Or you can be brutally honest about today while maintaining productive delusion about tomorrow.

High agency people: See clearly. Believe unreasonably. Act relentlessly.

Closing question:

Would it be okay if that started today?

Skill Four: Resilience

"If you're not failing, you're not pushing your limits, and if you're not pushing your limits, you're not maximizing your potential"

— Ray Dalio

Everyone gets knocked down. You have. I have. The question is: how fast do we get back up?

Resilience isn't about being the toughest in the room. It's about recovery time. The distance between impact and action.

Most people stay down for days, weeks, months. Some never get up.

High agency people have trained themselves to bounce back faster and come back stronger.

V-Shaped Recovery

Picture a graph of your performance after failure.

Low agency creates a U-shape. Long, flat bottom. Slow climb back. Sometimes never reaching original height.

High agency creates a V-shape. Sharp drop, sharper recovery. Often higher than before.

The difference isn't the fall — setbacks happen in anything worth pursuing. It's the bounce. The recovery rate. How fast you get back up.

It's Not About Feelings

Resilience isn't about not feeling the hit.

Of course you do. We all do. The sting of failure. The disappointment. The embarrassment. The urge to quit.

The difference is how fast you recover and not allowing them to determine your behavior longer than necessary.

Got rejected? Lost a big client? Launched something that tanked? It all hurts. But, recovery time matters. It's getting back in the ring faster while most people are still nursing their egos.

Adaptive Persistence

Resilience without adaptation is just stubbornness.

High agency resilience isn't about doing the same thing until it magically works. It's about learning, adjusting, and iterating.

Each failure sharpens your approach.

Each setback reveals something new.

Each rejection teaches you something.

You don't just get back up. You get back up smarter.

This is why you can fail 10 times and succeed on attempt 11. You're not doing the same thing repeatedly. You're iterating rapidly.

And all you need in business is one big win that makes it all worth it.

The Cosmic Perspective

Here's a mental model that's useful:

"Will this matter in 10 years? 10 months? 10 days?"

Probably not.

That "catastrophic" mistake? Nobody's going to remember.

A "devastating" rejection? Who cares?

That "career-ending" failure? Funny how those never last.

Think about the hours, days, or years low agency people spend worrying over things that don't matter?

Now, imagine if you got all that time back and applied to doing the thing you've been wanting to?

High agency people zoom out. See the cosmic irrelevance. Then get back to accomplishing their goals.

Building Your V

Here's a wild idea: you can apply **Parkinson's Law** to setbacks. In a nutshell — work shrinks or expands to the time available for it's completion.

Now, apply this to setbacks. By creating parameters, you limit the downside and create the upside.

Here's how that looks:

Minor setback? Cool. Give yourself 5 minutes to feel it. Then move on.

Medium failure? Take the afternoon. Then strategize.

Major disaster? Take the day. Then rebuild.

Each time, shrink the window. What took a week now takes a day. What took a day now takes an hour.

This is a skill that's trainable. High agency people have trained themselves to deal with setbacks differently and you can as well.

In life, winning often comes down to the person who doesn't give up.

Becoming Unstoppable

Learning to become more resilient isn't something we're taught in school. But, it's one of the most necessary skills if you want to do anything beyond your current capacity.

Most people don't treat it like it's trainable. Hopefully, I've shown you that it is.

And once you start building it, you become a force to be reckoned with.

The more resilient you are, the more swings at the bat you get. And sometimes all it takes is that 11th swing to hit something so big your entire life changes.

Start training it, and watch how fast you can do things you once thought were impossible.

Skill Five: Calibrated Thinking

Too many people get blindsided by reality — over and over.

The "sure thing" falls apart. The "perfect" hire turns out to be a disaster. The "foolproof" strategy turns out to be not so foolproof after all.

It's frustrating. And it's not just bad luck. It's a calibration problem.

Calibrated thinking — is your ability to notice signals, interpret what they mean, and adjust your behavior accordingly.

Said another way, calibrating is: reading signals and adjusting in real-time.

Many people don't do this. They seem to repeatedly get different flavors of the same problem.

Same boss, different company. Same relationship, different partner. Same failure, different packaging.

If you learn to calibrate, you break the loop so you're not facing the same boss over and over again.

In the short term, it looks like adaptability. Long-term, it turns into pattern recognition. This means you can anticipate and predict with greater accuracy.

A $40 Billion Signal

In 2000, Netflix pitched Blockbuster on a partnership. Reed Hastings offered to run Blockbuster's online brand for $50 million.

Blockbuster's CEO John Antioco literally laughed them out of the room.

Exit deal. Enter calibration:

Blockbuster saw that rejection as validation. "See? Online rentals are a joke. Stick with what works — late fees and retail stores."

Netflix saw it as a signal. The old guard wouldn't adapt. Opportunity to beat them on a changing landscape.

One company insisted their model was right and the market was wrong. The other calibrated to what the signal was telling them: the future wouldn't include video stores.

Blockbuster went from 9,000 stores to bankrupt in a decade. Netflix is worth $240 billion.

Netflix calibrated. Blockbuster didn't.

What This Actually Looks Like

Watch someone with calibrated thinking operate.

They're in a sales pitch. Halfway through, they completely change their approach. Why? They noticed the buyer's energy shift so they changed strategy.

They try something new. Week one shows it's not working as expected. Instead of forcing their original plan, they pivot to what's actually happening.

They meet someone everyone says is great. Something feels off. They trust that signal over the consensus.

They're always reading. Always adjusting. Never so attached to being right that they can't change course.

Ego Or Results?

Most people: "This should work" → doesn't work → "The market is wrong."

High agency: "This should work" → doesn't work → "What am I missing?"

One protects their ego. The other protects their results.

Pattern Recognition in Real Time

When you pay attention to signals others dismiss, you start seeing patterns.

You're able to create finer distinctions and spot problems before they arise.

The beautiful thing about pattern recognition is once you've seen enough, you're able to start predicting what will happen next. You can anticipate what's going to happen and adjust appropriately.

So many people continuously are solving old problems that are just dressed up in new clothes. You can get off that train and start creating outcomes at new levels because you're constantly calibrating.

Ethically Stealing

Why would you limit yourself to domain specific solutions? High agency people steal solutions from everywhere. I call it *cross-domain sourcing.*

Maybe they apply trading analysis to a construction business for greater arbitrage. Or you might apply Hollywood promotion strategies for product launches.

Whatever it is, there are solutions others have discovered that are just waiting to be applied to different areas of your life.

High agency doesn't care where solutions come from. It only cares about results and using whatever resources possible.

Reading Between The Lines

Calibrated thinking hears what's not being said. And believe me, this is a superpower. Here's how it looks:

> "I'm overwhelmed" → you hear "I don't know how to prioritize."

> Customer says "too expensive" → you hear "I don't see the value."

> Partner says "fine" → you hear "definitely not fine."

How can you expect to appropriately respond if you don't appropriately listen?

Reading the signals is the key. You have to respond to the real message, not the surface one.

Speed of Adjustment

The difference between someone who calibrates fast versus slow creates a huge gap in their results.

Low agency people take years to admit they're wrong. High agency people find out in days.

Not because they're less attached to being right. They love to win. But because they're more attached to getting results.

Calibrating means you're reacting and learning faster.

Wrong approach? Bad hire? Failed strategy? Better to know in days rather than months or years.

Specificity as a Weapon

Vagueness kills calibration.

You can't calibrate based on vague ideas. "I want to make more money" doesn't cut it.

How much more?

By when?

What would you have to do to make it unreasonable for you to fail?

Part of calibrating your thinking is specificity.

Vague thinking leads to vague results.

Calibrated thinking demands precision. You can't calibrate fuzzy.

Making Finer Distinctions

The better your distinctions, the better your calibration.

Most people hear "no" and think "rejection." But, you can train yourself to hear more types of no:

- "No, not now" (timing)
- "No, not from you" (wrong messenger)
- "No, not like that" (wrong approach)
- "No, too expensive" (price or value)
- "No, I don't understand" (clarity)

Each one requires a different adjustment. If you treat them all the same, you'll keep missing the mark.

With and Without Calibration

The gap between those who calibrate and those who don't keeps widening.

With calibration:

You catch problems while they're small. You see the signals early. You waste less time defending ideas that aren't working. You pivot fast. You find what works while others are still debating what should work.

Without it:

You hit the same walls repeatedly. Same mistakes, different day. You blame bad luck for predictable outcomes. "Why does this keep happening?" You follow advice that worked for someone else in a different situation. You're that person who keeps doing the same thing expecting different results.

It's like driving with GPS versus a 1995 map. One adjusts to the road in real time. The other has you driving into a lake saying, "But the map said road."

Building Calibration

Start here:

> Notice when reality surprises you. That's a calibration opportunity.

> Instead of explaining why reality is wrong, ask what signal you missed.

> Pay attention to people who get different results with the same resources. What are they seeing that you're not?

> Make finer distinctions so you can calibrate more specifically.

The Bottom Line

Smart people have good ideas. High agency people have good adjustments.

Your brilliant strategy means nothing if you can't adapt when it hits reality.

The world doesn't care about your theory. It only responds to what actually works.

Stop defending your first answer. Start finding the right answer.

That's calibrated thinking. Start noticing the signals. Understand what they mean. And adjust your behavior — fast.

Skill Six:
Creative Resourcefulness

Derek Sivers started CD Baby in his bedroom with $500.

No warehouse. No shipping department. No customer service team. Just a musician who needed to sell his CD online in 1998 when nobody else would do it.

By the time he sold it ten years later for $22 million, CD Baby had paid out over $100 million to 150,000 independent musicians.

How? Creative resourcefulness — seeing possibility where others see dead ends.

The Recognition Game

Learning to recognize present resources is a superpower.

The real real is that most people have far more resources than they recognize yet are recognition-poor.

We haven't been taught to play the game of life in the most efficient manner.

It's why two people can be stuck on an island and one builds a boat and the other uses the materials for a help sign. Same resources, different results.

Take Derek Sivers for instance. He didn't have what he "needed" to start a music distribution company.

He didn't have a warehouse or shipping system, or business model when starting.

So he used his bedroom, slipped in handwritten thank-you notes into the packages, and just copied the local consignment store's business model.

Was it genius or was it resourceful action?

A low agency trap is waiting for resources rather than creating them from what's already available.

Becoming The Person Who Always Figures it Out

We all know someone who finds a way despite circumstances.

Why is that?

Do they have some special skill that's unavailable to the rest of us?

No, they simply exercise greater resourcefulness. When there's an obstacle, they get creative while others accept it as a stop sign.

When you enjoy figuring things out and it becomes a puzzle worth solving, you get better at solving them.

And the more you solve, the better you get along the way.

This isn't about having all the answers. It's about your ability to actually discover and create the answers along the way.

It's why high agency people have a certain confidence about them. They don't have to know everything, they simply trust in their belief to find the answers to the problems presented.

Possibility Creation

Most people see two paths and that's the end. When you exercise creative resourcefulness you begin to realize more options always exist.

"We can't afford it" becomes "How could we afford it?"

"It's impossible" becomes "What would have to be true for this to work?"

"Either/or" becomes "What are five other ways this could be done?"

You don't have to be a genius either. It just takes a bit of creativity and letting yourself see that there are other paths available.

Every dead end is just a possibility for creativity.

Better Questions, Better Resources

The quality of your questions determines the resources you find.

Ask "Why me?" and your brain finds reasons you're a victim.

Ask "What can I learn from this?" and your brain finds lessons.

Or

Ask "Why don't I have enough?" and you'll be discouraged by comparison.

Ask "What can I create with what I have?" and you'll discover possibilities.

Questions are how you open to a world of possibilities. And these don't always feel rational. Sometimes you have to ask big, outlandish questions that generate seemingly insane results. But, there's usually a nugget of gold in there that will move you forward.

There's Always A Way

We're all at different places in life and have to work with what we've got. So many people have been resource poor and created a resource rich life simply by being more resourceful.

A low agency trap is to believe the story we tell ourselves about limited resources and allow ourselves to be victims to this.

The high agency solution is to practice creative resourcefulness and be unreasonable about what we're pursuing.

It's not always about the resources you have or don't have. It's how determined and resourceful you are to overcome whatever the obstacle in your path is.

Your creativity and insight can be some of your greatest resources.

Look, you'll never have perfect conditions. Sometimes you just have to start wherever you're at and make it work from there.

And there's always a way.

Skill Seven:
Frame Control

Out of all these skills, frame control may be the one I use most.

It's been the difference between me quitting or continuing countless times.

It's also been the difference in closing deals, helping people reframe their problems into possibilities, and creating lifelong relationships.

It's a *legit* superpower when you master it.

Frame control is choosing which story you tell about what happens to you.

Every situation has multiple valid interpretations. High agency people deliberately choose the one that drives the outcome they want.

Sounds simple, like everyone would do it. And they do. Just not always in service of results.

Low agency people may choose to find what *validates their victimhood* rather than what could bring them closer to a big goal.

You're always choosing. Frame control is simply taking control from an *outcome perspective*.

Lost a client? True. Also true: You just made room for a better one. Both are facts. Which one you focus on determines what happens next.

Outcome Drives The Frame

Frame control is choosing the frame that's most **useful** in moving you closer to your desired outcome.

Maybe it's more freedom, or financial security, or to close more sales.

You can't control everything but you can control what you allow things to mean.

I choose frames based on what's useful.

Frame Control For Challenges

As a coach, I look for patterns. What's the difference between someone who bounces back in days versus months or years?

A consistent theme is frame control. That's not to say there aren't plenty of other reasons, only that frame control is incredibly important. It might look like:

Same divorce — Both are heart-broken. But: One person frames it as abandonment and spirals for years. Another frames it as a gift for the time they had and starts their best chapter.

Two businesses fail — One sees proof they're a failure. Another sees an education in what doesn't work and how they can fix it in their next venture.

The events are similar but how each person chose to frame the content changes the context.

And the results over time create disproportionate outcomes.

A Parable Of Three Workers

Just to emphasize how important this is, here's a brief parable illustrating its power:

Three people work the same warehouse job.

Ask them what they do:

First: "I break my back for minimum wage. Life's unfair and I'm proof."

Second: "I provide for my family. It's honest work and I'm proud."

Third: "I'm learning logistics to start my distribution company. This is my free MBA."

Same job. Same pay. Same hours.

The first quits in six months, bitter.

The second stays twenty years, content.

The third launches their company in two years using everything they learned.

Here's the magic: The frame didn't just change their experience. **It predicted their future.**

And you have the ability to exercise control over this in your life.

The Four Levels of Frame Control

Frames are changeable — for yourself and others. Master these four levels and you'll be amazed at how fast things can change. Just watch.

Default frame: How you experience life.

"Everything is always wrong." or "How can I use this to move forward?"

Result: No results or more results.

Pre-frame: How you frame things before they happen.

"This dinner is going to be so fun."

Result: You set it up so it's more likely to be.

Re-frame: How you frame things afterwards.

"That horrible client taught me exactly who I won't work with from now on."

Result: Move forward faster with more experience.

De-frame: How you break the frame.

"Wait. Should we even be trying to solve this problem?"

Result: Avoid unhelpful frames.

High Agency Framing

Without frame control, you essentially just take whatever life throws at you.

With frame control, you control what it means and have greater resilience.

You can help others see possibilities they couldn't before. You can help create an atmosphere of trust rather than one of distrust.

Can you imagine someone dealing with rejection over and over again without being able to reframe it into something useful?

It's part of what separates those who push through difficulty in business and those who throw in the towel.

They're able to give a useful meaning to things rather than be beaten down by difficulty.

Expanding Frames for Others

Frame control isn't just for you. You can use it to help expand someone's perspective also.

When someone's stuck in a limiting frame, you can help them see other options.

Friend: "I got fired. I'm a failure."

You: "Or you just got paid to learn valuable skills and what environment doesn't work for you."

Employee: "This project is impossible."

You: "What would it look like if it were easy?"

Partner: "I'm stuck in my career."

You: "What if you highlighted your real skills and jumped 3 levels?"

You're showing them possibilities they can't see from inside their frame.

It's one of the kindest things you can do for another. To help them see the best parts of themselves we're all sometimes incapable of recognizing in ourselves.

High agency people naturally do this. They expand possibilities for others the same way they do for themselves. Not by denying reality, but by revealing options.

The person calling you from a hostile nation needs you to frame the situation as solvable, not hopeless. That's not delusional — that's useful.

Framing To Win

You're telling yourself stories all day. Every day.

The meeting you're dreading — you're already framing it.

The goal that feels impossible — you're already creating friction around it.

The conversation you've been putting off — you're building a story of how it's going to go.

High agency people ask a different question: Is this frame helping or hindering me?

If it's not helping you, change it.

The facts will be the facts.

But what you choose to do with them matters immensely.

When you learn to wield frame control in this way, you'll find opportunities you never knew existed.

Change your frame and you'll change your life.

Skill Eight: Connectable

You can be brilliant. You can be driven. You can have frame control down pat. But if you're not connectable, you're going to massively cap your ceiling.

Why? Because high agency doesn't operate in a vacuum. Individual agency has limits. Connection creates leverage.

One of the fastest ways I've seen people change their lives is simply being more connectable.

Opportunities flow through people. The job you want, the client you're chasing, the relationship that changes everything — they all come from someone else.

And here's the best part: you don't have to be "ready" or "qualified" before connection creates those doors. I've watched countless people with less skill or less experience leapfrog others just because they were more connectable.

Being Connectable

A misconception of being connectable is that it's only about charisma, or being liked, or being nice. While those things are great — you don't always like the person who's pushing you towards your potential.

They'll have the tough conversations you won't find with others. They may be uncomfortable in the moment, but you respect them, and find yourself better off for it.

Being connectable is being able to hold the space so that people have the opportunity to experience greater possibilities and growth.

It's creating genuine resonance with others.

High agency people are connectable because they:

- See people's potential, not just their current state
- Share energy rather than hoarding it
- Build relationships, not just transactions
- Make others feel capable, not inferior
- Create wins for everyone, not just themselves

This is why they can:

- Lead teams without formal authority
- Get help without asking
- Build trust without credentials
- Create movements without money

Enrollment Power

Think about the last time someone inspired you to act. Like really act.

They didn't just explain their idea. They *enrolled* you in it. Their certainty became your certainty. They showed you YOUR capability through that vision.

That's what enrollment is: energy transfer.

And it's one of the strongest skills of connectability you can build.

When you learn to enroll people, they won't just hear your vision — they start believing in themselves through it.

You'll find yourself saying things like:

"You could do this in your sleep."

"This lines up perfectly with how your brain works."

"I can already see you crushing this."

And this isn't meant to be blowing smoke. You're helping them see past their self-imposed limitations and to their actual capability.

Do that consistently, and people will move mountains to be around you.

Multiplication Through People

I've yet to meet a single person who built or accomplished anything significant alone.

Being connectable is key to operating with high agency.

The myth of the lone genius is exactly that — a myth. Every breakthrough required enrolled believers.

Jobs enrolled Wozniak. Wozniak enrolled engineers. Engineers enrolled the world.

High agency people build movements, not just businesses. They turn individual capability into collective force.

They get teams working for equity before there's a product. They get customers buying before there's inventory. They get investors writing checks before there's revenue.

How? They enroll them in tomorrow, not today.

They cast a vision so powerful and compelling that people ask, "How can I be a part of this?"

The Network Effect

The more you build this skill, the more your network starts working with you on a different level.

Opportunities start flowing your way that never did before. Introductions happen naturally. Resources start surfacing because people want to be a part of something they believe in.

It can look like luck to people on the outside. It's not. It's simply the power of genuine connection.

Connection Creates Capability

High agency people understand: Your individual capability is multiplied by your ability to connect.

The business owner who builds real relationships with employees gets extra effort. The manager who connects authentically gets innovation, not just compliance. The salesperson who genuinely connects closes deals competitors can't touch. Whether you're leading a team of 2 or 200, your ability to connect determines your ability to deliver.

The key is to genuinely care.

I know. What a concept.

In a world where everyone is "networking" or trying to climb some social ladder status game, the person who is connectable and adds value wins.

Where To Start

You don't need to be the most charismatic person in the room to be more connectable. Here's where to start:

Genuinely care. Not as a tactic — it's about principle. People can feel the difference.

See potential. Speak to who people can become, not just who they are now.

Transfer energy. Don't just explain with no emotion. Actually allow your conviction to bleed through. Others will feel it.

Create wins. Genuinely help others win and they'll help you win. Connection isn't some zero-sum game.

Connection Creates Leverage

Ideas don't change the world. People do.

Your vision is worthless if you can't enroll others to see it also. Your agency is limited if you're the only one using it.

Being connectable and enrolling others into a higher version of themselves leads to greater capability to solve problems and change the world.

That's the power of being connectable. Not just having agency yourself, but multiplying it through genuine connection with others.

The Highest Agency Bulldog

Meet Candler Cook.

It's fall of 2007, and he's a tall, scrawny freshman entering college at The University of Georgia (UGA).

And he has a secret: From the age of 7 he's wanted to be a UGA Bulldog. Not just a student — a football player.

The only problem is… everything.

UGA has one of the toughest football programs and teams in the entire nation. And he'd be trying to earn a walk-on position.

Statistically, you're more likely to be struck by lightning than earn a spot on the roster.

Challenge accepted.

Candler is unqualified in nearly every way possible except being a student.

He only weighs 145lbs and was one of the weakest and slowest kids on his high school team.

Not exactly college football material compared to the athletes who regularly graduate from UGA and are drafted into the NFL.

He gets to work.

No idea how to try out as a walk-on? He figures it out.

Too skinny? By Halloween he's up 25lbs and faster and stronger.

By the end of the semester, only 6 of the original 12 who wanted to walk-on were left.

Candler pushes through the off-season workouts and drills through the spring that often leave future-NFL players puking.

He's not the most gifted. Everyone can see it. He can see it. But he refuses to quit.

Then a week after the spring game, he's called into the coaches office with several others.

They were cut. The tryout was over and he didn't make it.

Resilience

Candler decided he wasn't going to stop.

He trained through the summer, working out six days a week, and eating more — determined to weigh 232 by December.

By October, he'd bulked up to 214lbs and massively increased strength.

Time to test his hard work.

Candler entered a UGA powerlifting competition called The Strongest Dawg.

Not only did he win his weight class, he also soared past all weight classes with the highest deadlift of the day.

What he was doing was working. Yet, he knew he needed more.

Time to increase the meals to 8x per day, or roughly every 2 hours.

If it sounds miserable, that's because it is.

He hit his target weight in December and secured another round at spring tryouts.

Even though he'd bulked up 87lbs, he still needed to increase his strength and speed.

Spring followed with more grueling training and drills and ended with the spring game.

A week later, he was cut — again.

To top disappointment off further, he found a disheartening review sheet with personal notes by one of the coaches.

The coach claimed he "must face facts," and "should strongly consider giving it up."

Gut punch.

Motivation

Most people might let this sort of disappointment stop them.

Candler used it as motivation and made copies of the review sheet.

He bumped up to 10 meals a day, consuming over 15,000 calories at one point, and trained even harder.

He also decided to switch from trying out as a linebacker to defensive end.

By January the next year, he was a new man from the scrawny 145lb kid who originally decided he wanted to be a bulldog. Now, he weighed in at 250lbs of solid muscle and athleticism.

This was his last tryout before his senior year. Even though he could still play as a 5th year senior he was driven by a near fanatical sense of urgency and hunger.

Candler knew he couldn't be just another guy through spring drills. He'd need to lead. So he did.

Another spring game came and went.

And for the third time, he got called into the coaches office.

But this time was different.

Upon leaving, he was now a UGA Bulldog.

He'd made it onto one of the most competitive college football teams in the world.

Now, he'd have to work even harder to ensure he wasn't simply on the team — but claimed his spot on the field, in a game.

1543 Days

Candler trained over the summer and made it through fall practices.

The scout team mainly helped the starters but was an opportunity for him to get a lot of reps in.

Reps he needed if he was going to play in a game.

Despite all his efforts, he never got an opportunity to play during his first season as a Bulldog.

He could've thrown in the towel and settled with having made the team. But he wasn't going to do that.

The season ended and he was back training in the spring. Again.

Candler knew this was his last shot and gave everything he had.

Spring and summer went by with the same relentless training and his last season arrived.

The team entered a winning streak and Candler knew this was his chance.

Rather than simply trust fate, he told his coach if the opportunity opened, he wanted to play in the New Mexico State game.

Two days later, with only 5:51 left in the game, Candler rushed onto the field.

It had been 1,543 days since he'd first walked into the coaches office to ask about trying out.

Every Skill In One Story

Candler went from life happening to him to happening to life.

He might be the highest agency Bulldog who's ever lived.

His story demonstrates just how crucial and powerful these different skills are to operating with high agency.

Candler's journey from a skinny 145lb kid to UGA Bulldog isn't about athletic ability. It's about high agency in action.

Watch how the skills compound:

His *obsession* made him eat 10 meals a day. *Strategic non-conformity* let him ignore "give it up." *Brutal honesty* showed him he needed 100+ more pounds. *Productive delusion* convinced him it was possible.

Resilience brought him back after being cut twice. *Calibrated thinking* made him switch from linebacker to defensive end when the first approach failed. *Creative resourcefulness* had him eating during exams to hit his meal targets. *Frame control* turned a crushing evaluation into motivation fuel.

And being *connectable* got him the training partners, extra chances, and respect that kept doors open.

Remove any one skill and the story ends with a skinny kid who "faced facts."

Together, they turned impossibility into inevitability.

Not through talent. Through compounding high agency.

Every skill pulling in the same direction. Every rejection becoming data. Every obstacle becoming a puzzle. Every "no" becoming "not yet."

1,543 days of all eight skills working together.

Like those Belgian horses pulling together — one skill might move you forward, but all eight in sync? That's when impossible weights start moving.

That's how a 145-pound kid with no business being on a football field became a Bulldog.

And that's how impossible happens.

Your Impossible Goal

What impossible thing are you not pursuing?

Which of the skills would you need to turn the dial up on to make that impossible goal inevitable?

You don't need all eight at 10/10. You just need them all pulling together.

The distance between where you are and where you want to be isn't talent or luck. It's behavior. And extraordinary results come from turning these skills into action.

SECTION III: APPLICATION

Escaping Low Agency Traps

High agency people who are stuck living low agency lives are often stuck in a series of traps.

How do you know when you're stuck in one of these traps?

You're working hard but going nowhere.

Busy but not building. Moving but not progressing. Trying but not succeeding.

The most difficult part is that these traps *feel* productive. That's what makes them so dangerous. You think you're doing something when you're actually doing nothing.

The worst part? They only exist in your mind. They're a sort of self-imposed mental prison where you're both the guard and prisoner.

How to Spot a Trap

Simple: You're not getting the results you want.

More subtle: You're getting small results that prevent big ones.

Even subtler: You're comfortable with your excuses.

If you flipped the eight high agency skills upside down, you'd have the perfect recipe for staying stuck forever.

No obsession, just mild interest.

No strategic non-conformity, just outsourcing your sense of self.

No frame control, just accepting whatever meaning is handed to you.

"Faced with the choice of changing one's mind and proving there is no need to do so, almost everyone gets busy on the proof."

— John Kenneth Galbraith

Low agency people would rather defend their limitations than escape them.

There are countless low agency traps and even more ways to escape them.

The first step to escape any trap is recognizing you're stuck in one (brutal honesty).

Once you identify you're stuck in one, escaping becomes infinitely easier. Most people stay stuck in them so long simply by not acknowledging they're stuck in one.

Below are several common traps with potential escape plans.

The Special Snowflake Trap

"But for me it's different..."

I know. Your problems are unique. Your situation is special. The thing that worked for everyone else won't work for you because [insert elaborate explanation about your childhood, your brain, your circumstances, your zodiac sign].

You've built an identity around being the exception. The one for whom normal rules don't apply. It's not ego - it's worse. It's reverse ego. You're special in your inability.

The tell: You start sentences with "Yeah but in my case..." and end them with why you can't.

Escape Route: Stop being the exception who can't. Start being the exception who does. Your circumstances might be unique. The principles that create results aren't. Gravity works on everyone.

The Sophistocrat Trap

"That's too simple to work..."

The sophistocrat trap plagues people at all levels. Some things need to be complex. But complex before they're ready? Doing the right things in the wrong order makes them wrong.

Put the bolts on before you install the tire and it doesn't work.

A low agency trap is to need complex systems, sophisticated strategies, nuanced approaches when simple is better.

I know. The obvious solution? That's for average minds. Basic people do basic things.

The sophistocrat confuses complexity with intelligence. They'd rather fail brilliantly than succeed obviously. They'd rather be intellectually interesting than actually effective.

The simple solution feels like cheating. Like you didn't earn it. If it's not hard, it doesn't count. So you add layers, frameworks, methodologies until the simple becomes impossible.

Meanwhile, someone with half your IQ is succeeding with the obvious approach you dismissed.

The tell: Your explanation takes longer than doing it would. You've spent more time designing your system than using it. You can explain why everything won't work but can't show anything that has.

Escape route: What's the dumbest solution that might work? Try that first. You can always add sophistication to something that exists. You can't add existence to something sophisticated.

The Prepper's Trap

"I just need to know one more thing..."

You've read 47 books on writing but haven't written a page. Watched every YouTube video on starting a business but haven't registered an LLC. You're collecting tactics like Pokemon cards, thinking the next one will finally make you ready.

It's the personal trainer paradox: "I'll hire a trainer once I'm in shape."

The driving lesson logic: "I'll take lessons once I know how to drive."

You're waiting to be good before you practice being good.

The tell: Your browser has 73 open tabs of "ultimate guides" but your project folder is empty.

Escape route: Do first, learn what you need when you need it. Spend 90% of time doing, 10% learning just-in-time information. You don't need step 37 before taking step one.

The Meta-Trap

The fun part about all these? They're all the same trap.

They're stories. Mental movies. Elaborate explanations for why you can't do simple things.

- Snowflake: "I'm too unique for normal solutions"
- Sophistocrat: "I'm too smart for simple solutions"
- Prepper: "I'm not ready for any solutions"

None of this is real. It's all happening between your ears.

In reality, there's just the thing to do and whether you do it or not. The rest is mental commentary.

Someone stuck in these traps can explain for hours why they can't start. The high agency move is to simply start.

The trap isn't your circumstances or intelligence or readiness. The trap is believing the story you're telling yourself about why you can't act.

Reality Is The Cure

The Wright Brothers didn't think their way to flight. They built wings and crashed. Built better wings and crashed better. Each crash taught them what thinking never could.

That's the pattern: High agency people make contact with reality. Low agency people make contact with their thoughts about reality.

One produces results. The other produces reasons.

The Escape

People break free when they stop believing their own stories.

When they realize the elaborate explanation for why they can't is just noise.

When they understand that all their thinking is just avoiding the simple act of starting.

The gap between low and high agency is the gap between your head and your hands. Between the story and the action. Between thinking about the thing and touching the thing.

Every trap has the same escape: Stop telling yourself stories about why you can't. Start doing.

Breaking The Pattern

Watch someone escape low agency. They don't get smarter. They don't get stronger. They don't get luckier.

They just stop believing their own excuses.

One day they realize their elaborate explanation for why they can't is just noise. Their brilliant analysis of the problem IS the problem.

So they do something. Anything. Maybe badly. But they do it.

And that small, imperfect action teaches them more than years of perfect thinking.

Next Steps

Momentum starts with behavior change.

If you feel stuck in any trap: Do something different. Not tomorrow. Not when you're ready. Today.

It doesn't have to be good. It doesn't have to be perfect. It just has to be real. It just needs to move you outside of fantasy land into action.

Climbing The High Agency Ladder

High agency isn't just an idea — it's behavior that creates results.

This goes beyond mindset. Beyond theory. It's the actual doing that makes the difference.

Figuring It Out

That business person who seems like a wizard? They exercised high agency to get there. They didn't start with better information — they acted their way to it.

Most of the successful people you admire aren't successful because they were somehow born different or special. They're successful because they continually climbed up the high agency ladder.

It's helpful to study what they did to develop those behaviors, not just where they are now. Most spent years building these skills. They *conditioned* behavior that now looks automatic.

They weren't always motivated or convinced things would work out. Many that I know spent years listening to motivation in the morning just to push through another day. It's not always sexy but it gets results.

The unsexy truth to a sexy life is that you have to condition behavior before it becomes automatic. And that conditioning process isn't always easy or fun but the other side is beyond worth it.

Climbing Rungs

The reality of climbing up the high agency ladder is that it never stops. You don't even know how high it or you can go. It's like climbing up a ladder covered in fog. You can't see how many rungs are left. You just know each one brings new challenges and greater rewards.

The reality with people who think they've peaked is that they've stopped climbing the ladder. And taking a break is different than getting off the ladder all together.

Self-surrender is peak low-agency.

The key thing to remember is that these skills aren't built through contemplation. They're built in the field, through action that forces them to emerge and strengthen.

To reiterate — Knowing and doing are universes apart.

You likely know enough to take step one — or to find out how. That's all you need. Just-in-time information beats just-in-case preparation.

My goal has been to hopefully nudge you a bit further up the ladder and also to show you the skills required to keep going further.

High Agency Capability

High agency isn't about being "on" all the time. It's being capable of turning it on when you need it. I know plenty of high performers who crush it in business and also occasionally go and let loose.

There's no 'right' way. It's not about perfection. It's about having the capability to actively shape your life and circumstances regardless of obstacles.

I've struggled through countless challenges in my life. Failed businesses. Relationship crash and burns. Social isolation. Peers betting against me. Not knowing how to do some impossible thing that I was determined to do anyway.

Every single time, I had to exercise agency to reach the next rung. Sometimes barely hanging on, sometimes climbing confidently. But always climbing.

At 37, it feels like I have several lifetimes worth of stories because I refuse to give in. I refuse to passively accept the world as I'm told it is.

Knowing Isn't Demonstrating

You don't need to know about high agency to demonstrate it. People have done this throughout history without naming it.

But having a roadmap helps. Like swimming — you can figure it out through trial and error, or you can learn technique and go further, faster.

Taking greater control over your life and circumstances is one of the greatest gifts you can give yourself and the world.

This book isn't meant to be the last book on high agency. It's meant to be a bridge to help you climb up the ladder. To get you taking action and control over life so that you start getting the high agency results you want.

Don't be the world's best kept secret because you 'know' about high agency yet fail to demonstrate it.

The Missing Link

High agency may just be the most important missing link in whatever it is you're trying to achieve or do.

You probably already demonstrate high agency in some areas. The parent who always figures out how to provide. The employee who solves problems others avoid. The friend everyone calls in crisis.

Now is the time to consciously and intentionally expand it.

Pick your weakest skill from the eight. Commit to one action this week that forces it to grow.

The world needs more people who don't need permission, who figure things out, who make things happen. More humans who've learned to trust their ability to figure things out because they do.

That's high agency. That's what you're building.

Your next rung awaits.

The Importance Of Speed

I wasn't going to include this chapter but decided to at the last minute.

There's no shortage of people with their opinions on high agency. The only thing I look at is — how do I implement this to get results?

You may be left asking yourself: But how do I apply these 8 skills to create outcomes today?

All the value is in the application. It's in the specific application of these skills to whatever lies between you and what you're trying to do.

And speed matters.

I decided to include this because high agency doesn't operate in a vacuum.

You don't have to figure everything out alone and high agency people especially try to shortcut their learning curves. Said another way, they prefer to pay to close the gap on their ignorance debt because it's usually far cheaper than figuring it out on their own.

Whether they hire coaches, consultants, trainers, better employees — whatever it is — they all use resources to speed up progress or to shrink the gap faster.

Breaking The Frame

Everyone says "only work with someone who's done exactly what you want to do."

The reality is: It depends.

Steve Jobs had Bill Campbell, a football coach, as his business advisor. Mark Zuckerberg hired Roger Federer's coach for personal performance. Oprah credits her success to multiple coaches throughout her journey.

Why would these people have advisors or coaches who haven't done what they're trying to do? I'll even take it a step further:

Bill Belichick never played professional football. He's still the greatest coach in NFL history.

Tony Robbins wasn't a trader when he coached Paul Tudor Jones to breakthrough performance.

None of these coaches had done what their clients were doing but still managed to help get them outsized results.

To be clear — there's absolutely a time and place for specialized knowledge. That's not the point.

The point is they provided an outside perspective, pattern recognition, and accountability.

It's difficult to see the picture when you're stuck inside the frame.

The Speed Advantage

Time is the only asset you can't create more of.

High agency people understand this. That's why they don't operate in isolation — they buy speed.

They hire coaches, consultants, trainers. Not because they can't figure things out alone, but because they value time and results over ego. Why spend 5 years trying to solve a problem yourself that someone else has already solved if you can just buy the solution?

Shrinking The Gap

Sometimes you need specialized knowledge — the exact blueprint for your exact situation.

More often, you need someone to:

- See the constraint you're blind to
- Create stakes that force action
- Provide frameworks you didn't know existed
- Call you on the stories you tell yourself

The value isn't always in new information. Sometimes it's just honest feedback from someone who is invested in calling you on your excuses and getting you results.

The Human Problems

I see people every day who could be given the perfect roadmap yet still get stuck. Why?

Because human problems oftentimes kill more dreams than strategic problems:

- Fear dressed up as "research"
- Perfectionism disguised as "standards"
- Comfort zones labeled as "being realistic"
- Ego protecting itself with complexity

A specialized expert can give you the map. But you might need someone to help you navigate the human maze that prevents you from following it.

It's not an either/or. It's both/and.

What Actually Moves People Forward

I've found people need different things at different times:

Sometimes it's *strategy* — seeing the move they're not seeing, the leverage point they're missing, the approach that changes everything.

Sometimes it's *structure* — frameworks for decision-making, systems for execution, models for thinking through complexity.

Sometimes it's *stakes* — external accountability that makes action non-negotiable, someone who won't accept their comfortable excuses.

Sometimes it's simply *perspective* — an outside view that reveals blind spots, challenges assumptions, or confirms what they suspected but couldn't articulate.

The constant is this: High agency people don't operate in isolation. They leverage everything available to accelerate their progress.

Climb Faster

Whichever way you choose to proceed, I'd encourage you to consider speed as an unfair advantage.

When you can climb faster than your competition — you win.

The highest agency people leverage every resource available.

They're not too proud to get help with strategy. Not too independent to benefit from structure. Not too strong to need stakes.

The ladder keeps going up. The only question is how fast you want to climb.

Next Steps

As much as I'd like to tell you I wrote this book in 30 days, the reality is it's taken years of building the very skills that made it possible. I hope the countless hours I've put into this work results in you getting outcomes beyond your wildest dreams.

I wouldn't be able to write books like this without you. So, if you're still here with me, thank you. It means the world to me. You're the best!

If you enjoyed this book, here are some more goodies so it doesn't have to end here:

1) **If you're struggling to determine your level of agency** — find out where you're at right now in a 5-minute quiz. It's free. HighAgencyHQ.com/freequiz.

2) **If you're struggling to track your daily high agency skills** — here's a free tracker: highagencyhq.com/dailytracker.

3) **Stay Connected** — Want more resources or to go deeper on high agency? Sign up here: highagencyhq.com/connected. I'll keep you in the loop about opportunities, events, courses, and other fun things.

4) **If you enjoyed this book or found it valuable** — I'd love to hear about it. Send me an email at: Caelin@HighAgencyHQ.com — I read every one personally.

Work With Me

If you'd like to explore working together — whether coaching, speaking, or other collaborations — email

Caelin@CaelinKompass.com with subject: **RESULTS**. I read every message personally.